FHM PRESENTS...

OUT OF THE MOUTHS OF
BABES

THIS IS A CARLTON BOOK

Text copyright © Emap Elan Network 2006
Design copyright © Carlton Books Limited 2006

This edition published by Carlton Books Limited 2006
20 Mortimer Street
London W1T 3JW

A CIP catalogue record for this book
is available from the British Library.

ISBN 13: 9-781-84442-316-3
ISBN 10: 1-84442-316-6

The material in this book was previously published in
FHM Presents... True Stories 2

Printed in Singapore

FHM PRESENTS...

OUT OF THE MOUTHS OF
BABES

CARLTON
BOOKS

Thanks to FHM's readers for all their true stories

www.fhm.com

HOMING INSTINCT

The missus was driving us home on the M1, northbound – except that when I glanced up from my newspaper I saw we were approaching the M25. When asked to explain why we'd gone 20 miles in the wrong direction, she sheepishly replied, "I thought we were going north because we were travelling uphill…"

BIT OF A BLOOMER

After constant nagging, I bought my wife a breadmaker. Eyeing the instructions, she turned to me in disappointment and said, "I didn't realise it needed ingredients as well." Silly me – I'd only gone and bought the non-magic version.

STRANGE BEDFELLOWS

Watching *Saving Private Ryan* with a few friends, my sister wandered in, waited patiently for a few minutes, then asked, "Which side are the Germans fighting for – the Nazis or the Americans?"

SHEER BAD LUCK

During the Golden Jubilee celebrations, my sister-in-law said what a shame it was that the Queen's dad had died just before she was crowned.

NO PRIZES FOR GUESSING

Playing 20 Questions during a long train journey, my girlfriend had to guess I was thinking of Freddie Mercury. She couldn't even work out what industry he was in, so as a not-so-subtle hint I started playing with my Walkman. "I get it!" she squealed. "Is it the man who invented headphones?"

TOWERING GENIUS

Walking past a building site, I mused out loud as to how such large cranes were built. My always-helpful girlfriend chipped in with, "If I was building one of those I'd start at the top and work down." Genius.

IN A LATHER

While I was driving our admittedly filthy motor
past a car-wash, my fiancée decided that enough
was enough and demanded I put it through the
"dishwasher". Then, on realising her mistake, she told
me never to send her faux pas "to MFI". No problem.

TWICE AS NICE

In Paris, me and the missus went on the Ferris wheel,
enabling me to point out the Eiffel Tower. "What's the
other tower over there?" asked the wife – pointing at
the reflection in a glass building.

GLASS ACT

Told by a casualty nurse that they'd had to remove a bottle from a guy's back passage, my naive mother-in-law asked, "How did he swallow that, then?"

DECEPTIVELY SPACIOUS

Chilling at my mate's house, one of his sister's friends asked to see the new conservatory. On viewing it, she exclaimed, "Wow! It's like a whole different room!"

THAT'S A TOUGHIE

At a party, we were playing "Six Degrees Of Kevin Bacon" – connecting any movie to the eponymous film star through six actors or fewer. My girlfriend set me a tough one: Footloose. Starring, er, Kevin Bacon.

IT HELPS

Approaching Glasgow Airport in the car last year, my wife was getting excited at the prospect of flying. "Wow!" she exclaimed. "Aren't the planes low when they're coming in to land?"

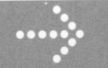

RUM DO

Ordering drinks on holiday, my girlfriend asked for a Margarita. I suggested getting a pitcher. "I can't," she replied, "The camera's in the apartment."

OH, SILLY ME

On Gran Canaria with my girlfriend, I noticed a man doing a spot of paragliding. "I bet he's having a great time up there in the thermals," I said. "Don't be stupid," she replied. "I'm sure they wear wetsuits."

I KNOW THE FACE...

A colleague of mine looked puzzled the other day. "Who plays Clint Eastwood?" she asked. "Is it Harrison Ford?"

DR WHO?

When a TV trail for *Dr Zhivago* came on, my wife said how sweet it was that they'd made a series about the man who started all those children's homes. She had a confused look when I explained about that nice Dr Barnardo.

SUCH A BEAUTIFUL LANGUAGE

On holiday recently in Mexico, we got chatting to a couple in the bar and discovered they were from Austria. "Oh, wow!" said my girlfriend. "Do you speak Ostrich?"

FHM

THANKS FOR THAT

Doing a crossword last week, my girlfriend asked to join in – so I read out "Biblical giant" as a clue. "Jolly Green!" she replied, quick as a flash.

SMALL WORLD

After telling my mum that a mate was on holiday in Kuala Lumpur, she replied, "Aren't they the little people in *Charlie and the Chocolate Factory*?"

I HEARD THAT TOO

One of my lovely girlfriend's colleagues was reviewing a book by immobile computer-voiced physicist Stephen Hawking. Stumped on the first sentence, she asked my girlfriend, "Is he American?" "He's English," she replied. The girl wasn't sure, and said, "I've seen him on TV and he's got an American accent."

TRAFFIC FLOW

Preparing for a road trip, my sister looked up from the map to declare, "I didn't know there was a river all the way round London." That'll be the M25.

NEVER MIND

When I asked the woman behind the newsagent's counter recently whether they had any Fisherman's Friends, she made a beeline for the magazine rack. "I can't see it here – but we've got *Angler's Week*, *Trout And Salmon*…"

LONG HOURS CULTURE

It'd been a hard day at work, when my colleague
Michelle asked me what the time was. "4.45,"
I replied. "Blimey!" she said. "It was six o'clock this
time yesterday."

DUMBER SUMMER

Listening to a report on the radio about the summer solstice, my girlfriend Lucy asked, "What's the solstice got to do with druids? Aren't they those little robots out of *Star Wars*?"

SMART THINKING

Driving into town, I had to stop at a railway crossing. As the barrier closed, my girlfriend's mate asked why there was a bell ringing. "So blind drivers know when to stop," replied my lovely girlfriend.

P

METRE MAIDS

I recently overheard one of our three secretaries asking, "How many kilos in a kilogram?" What's worse is that the other two didn't know either.

THAT'S HANDY

Walking past the Greenwich Observatory, my sister helpfully pointed out, "That was where time was invented."

ULTIMATE CHALLENGE

I was telling my girlfriend that I had a mate running the London Marathon, and that he was planning to participate in the Belfast one too. "Is that longer than London's?" she asked.

CONTINENTAL DRIFT

Driving the old girl down the A5, a motorbike with German registration went flying past. "I wonder if that's left-, or right-hand drive?" mused my mum.

OFF THE MAP

Overhearing a discussion about the supermarket chain Iceland changing its name to The Big Food Group, our female admin clerk at work commented, "That's a strange name for a country."

BOARD STUPID

While I was sanding down a piece of wood my girlfriend watched, amazed. "I didn't know that wood was made from little pieces of dust," she explained afterwards.

RITE OF SPRING

My girlfriend and I were talking about doing a bungee jump. I wondered whether they lowered the rope down when the jump was over, or winched you back to the top. My girl replied, "Don't you jump, bounce up and land on the platform again?"

TALKING BARBIE

We were having a barbecue in our friend Cathy's back garden, and the wind was blowing smoke into the kitchen. "Can't you turn the barbie around?" asked Cathy. "Then the smoke would blow the other way."

NOT APPLICABLE

My girl was filling in an application for holiday work. "Are you a member of a professional organisation?" asked one question. "Does that mean the IRA?" said my girlfriend.

SMALL BUT POWERFUL

Recently, I was cravenly trying to justify to my girlfriend why I was shelling out for a new car stereo system. I told her it featured a television, satellite navigation and a DVD player. "Cool," she replied. "It sounds like the bee's bollocks."

SOUNDS PLAUSIBLE

Surprised to read that raindrops only fall at 7mph,
I wanted to know what my girlfriend would guess.
"They come down from quite high…" she mused, "so
maybe a few thousand miles per second?"

GOD, YOU'RE RIGHT!

On holiday, during dinner, a girl at my table pointed out that it felt like we were moving. We were on a cruise.

NOT SO BAD

Out walking on a hot summer's day with my girlfriend, we saw some bin-men lugging dripping bags of rubbish across the road. "I don't fancy their job…" I commented. "Yeah, but they only work one day a week," she replied.

LEGENDARY HELLRAISER

Watching the news with my wife, it was announced that, sadly, Richard Harris had died. "What will happen to Orville?" my beloved wailed.

DELIBERATE MISTAKE

Watching that great British zombie flick *28 Days Later*, my beautiful young lady got agitated at the point in the film where we see a wind farm. "If there ain't any electricity," she piped up, "how come those wind turbines are going around?"

DO PAY ATTENTION

Reading an article on Princess Di, my girl came to a part about "her brother, Charles Spencer". "I thought her brother's name was Earl," she said.

FHM

THAT'S CLEVER

After watching Japan v Belgium, my friend turned over to the next match on a different channel, which kicked off ten minutes later. "That's amazing!" his girlfriend said. "How did they get the fans from the last game out and the new fans in so fast?"

SADLY NOT

A former girlfriend was always trying to take a photo of the beautiful sunsets on Ascension Island, but most evenings was foiled by the weather. "Doesn't the sun ever set in front of the clouds?" she asked me eventually.

NATURAL SELECTION

Watching dolphins in Singapore last year, my girlfriend was mightily impressed by their ability to perform complex tricks. "Well, they are the second most intelligent creatures on Earth," I replied, sagely. "What's the first?" she said, then pondered the answer for a moment: "The dog?" It appears so.

SENSE OF PROPORTION

On our descent into Dublin airport at 25,000ft, my wife pointed down at the bay. "You can see the fish jumping!" she said with girlish glee. Sadly, I had to inform her that she was looking at ferries.

IN A WAY, YES

Watching *Big Brother* with a female friend, we wondered where Cameron came from. I said he was from the Outer Hebrides. "Aren't they in space?" she said, puzzled.

TUBULAR BELLE

On a jolly to New Brighton, me and my good lady passed through the Mersey Tunnel from Liverpool to Birkenhead. My wife got all giddy. "This is good!" she said. "Is there one of these in Birkenhead as well?"

RUNNING ON EMPTY

Me and the missus noticed an old motor in a car park. "It's been there so long, it's sunk into the tarmac!" she said. It had four flat tyres.

BAG A BARGAIN

Discussing fake IDs, a mate said you could get a good one via the black market. "What day's that on?" asked my girl.

GLAZING OVER

Arriving at Heathrow, my sister squealed with excitement on seeing the air traffic control tower. "Oooh!" she exclaimed. "I've never seen a lighthouse before!" She's studying law at university.

NEARLY AS GOOD

My current girlfriend's sister had a summer job in a department store. I asked if that meant she got a discount. "No," my girl replied, "although she does only pay three-quarters of the price."

THAT'S THE BLOKE

On a day out in London my girlfriend came out with:
"You know the Nelson on Nelson's Column – is it
Nelson Mandela?"

P= said
Cheeky Monkey

CAN'T BE TOO CAREFUL

While at a friend's house, her mate came in, unplugged the phone and jacked her own phone in. "I'm expecting an important phone call," she explained.

WORTH A TRY...

Playing Risk with my housemate's girlfriend, I complained about the low numbers I was getting. "Try rolling the dice one at a time," she told me in all seriousness. "That way they won't affect each other."

HENCE THE NAME

Visiting Ireland recently, a friend took the wife and I on a coastal tour. "They call this U-Boat Rock," he told us. "It looks more like a submarine," replied the wife, quick as a flash.

WHO INDEED?

On a recent trip to the beach my now ex-girlfriend noticed a sign that read, "ALL REFUSE TO BE PUT IN BIN." "That's a stupid sign," she said, puzzled. "Who would agree to be put in a bin?"

NO ONE'S ASKING YOU TO

During a recent conversation with my dear old mum, we stumbled into the subject of homosexuality. "I couldn't be gay," she said. "I just couldn't have one of them things shoved up my arse."

OBVIOUS ANSWER

On a night flight back from Florida, my wife looked out of the window at the featureless sky and said, "Are we flying above the stars?" D'oh!

HIGH FLYER

One weekend, my sister's boyfriend announced that he intended to try out his new kite. "Don't be silly," my sister remarked, "it's too windy to fly a kite."

HOBBITOSAURUS

Watching *Lord Of The Rings* with the family, my 17-year-old sister asked, "When were all the creatures from Middle Earth around? Was it before or after the dinosaurs?"

BETWEEN THE STICKS

When the Ireland vs Spain World Cup game went to penalties, my girlfriend asked what would happen if both teams kept scoring. I told her that they go through all the players – even the goalkeepers. "Then who would save it?" she asked.

HIGH-MAINTENANCE

While driving to work, my partner looked out at the local school's all-weather hockey pitch, before turning to me and asking, "How often do you have to cut Astroturf?"

NATURE'S WAY

Sitting round the breakfast table, my sister stared at the bottle of milk before asking how farmers could tell the difference between semi-skimmed and full-cream cows.

IT'S A MYSTERY

During a school trip to a small island a few years ago my sister and I ate our packed lunches together, which attracted loads of greedy birds. "How did they get to the island?" my sis blurted out.

FAMILY TIES

During the Jubilee weekend my girlfriend piped up,
"Why does Prince Charles always hang around with
the Queen?" When I'd picked myself off the floor, she
confirmed that she hadn't realised the two were related.

SPEAKA DA LINGO

Out for dinner at a smart Spanish restaurant, my girlfriend made sure we didn't come over as ignorant tourists when she deftly greeted the waiter with, "Buenos Aires, señor!"

POWERFUL INSIGHT

One night the electricity went off. "It's definitely a power cut," I told the missus, looking out at the street in blackness. "It can't be," she informed me. "All the passing cars still have their lights on."

YUK YUK YUK

Watching *Who Wants To Be A Millionaire?*, the question, "Which Biblical character was famed for his enormous strength?" came up. "Popeye!" exclaimed the missus.

AD BRAKES

Riveted by the Grand Prix live on telly the other week, my girlfriend sent the entire room into hysterics by commenting, "Do they stop racing when the adverts come on?" Sad but true.

ASCENT OF MAN

On *The Life Of Mammals*, David Attenborough closed with: "Next week the story of the apes, and how one large primate took over the world." My watching girlfriend replied with, "Who's that; King Kong?"

DON'T TOUCH THAT DIAL

My father bought an antique wireless radio. Showing it to my girlfriend of the time, he explained that it needed to warm up, before tuning it in to Radio One. "Oh my God!" exclaimed my woman, bewitched. "It plays modern music!"

I DON'T GET IT

Trying to impress a female colleague with the wonders of the internet, I popped her postcode into an aerial mapping website and zoomed down on to her house. Bemused, she asked how come she could see her car sitting in the drive when it was clearly parked in our car park. Laugh? I nearly sacked her.

MISSING THE POINT

Watching a TV show about rhinos having their horns cut off to protect them from poachers, my lady housemate said, "That's terrible. How do they kill their prey?"

CRUMBS!

My sister-in-law asked what type of bread was most healthy, to which I replied "Brown." "I don't have any," she said. "Can't I just toast some white bread?"

IDIOT BOX

My (sadly) ex-girlfriend used to delight in watching trashy afternoon TV – until one afternoon when her flow of garbage was replaced by live coverage of a major sporting event. "Not again," she complained. "I'm going to have to buy another telly."

JUST ADD... ER...

A female friend of mine recently moved into a house where the fridge didn't work, so her dad bought her some dried milk. "How do I use this with cornflakes?" she asked me. "Do I sprinkle it on?" Brilliant.

EASY MISTAKE

During a visit to Chessington World of Adventures with my girlfriend, we found ourselves watching a lion. I jokingly mentioned that it looked like the roaring one at the beginning of MGM films. "That's the most famous lion in the world," replied my girlfriend. "Except for Tony the Tiger, of course."

WIDE VEHICLE

My father couldn't decide whether to sell his personalised numberplate or transfer it from his car on to his motorcycle. "Won't it stick out on either side?" chipped in my sister.

SEE? IT WORKS!

Out shopping with my girlfriend, we bought a copy of *The Big Issue*. The vendor told us it was his last one. "You can go home now," my girl informed him, helpfully.

TURNED OUT NICE AGAIN

Watching George Foreman flogging his "lean, mean, grilling machine" on TV, my girlfriend chipped in with: "What does he know about cooking? He plays the banjo."

ER... YES...

Seeing a live penguin for the first time, my girlfriend was amazed how small it was. "I'd always assumed they were my height," she explained.

WRONG NUMBER

Reading "Out Of The Mouths Of Babes" recently, my girlfriend asked, "What's 'WWII' mean?" I told her they were Roman numerals. "Were the Romans involved in World War Two?" she replied.

STICKY WICKET

In the pub, I asked my girlfriend's friend if she could tell me the cricket score, as my view of the TV was obscured. "Seventeen-nil!" she proudly exclaimed.

YOU COULDN'T MAKE IT UP

Me and a few workmates were coming out with various crap double entendres. Listening in, a female colleague blurted out: "I don't know what double entendres are – will one of you fill me in?"

NICE DOGGIES...

Watching the Stallone movie *Cliffhanger* on TV the other night, we came to the part where a man is hanging from a tree as a pack of hungry hounds nibble on his shoe. My lovely girlfriend innocently asked, "Are they rescue wolves?"

COME BACK LATER

Walking with my girlfriend along the seafront the other day, she came over all moody. "When I was a kid, this beach seemed huge," she reminisced. I had to spoil her musings by pointing out that the tide was in.

COMING IN TO LAND

Watching *Executive Decision* with my girlfriend, we came to the part where the two planes were hooked together. After popping out to answer a call of nature, I asked her what had happened in my absence. "The pilot ejaculated," she answered innocently.

ALL AT SEA

With news of a cyclone in the Solomon Islands, I suggested to my wife they should build underground shelters. "They can't!" she replied. "They're in the middle of the ocean – dig down and you spring a leak."

FATHER, FORGIVE THEM

My housemate read a fashion feature about how everyone was wearing crosses these days. "I've worn one for ages!" she exclaimed. I pointed out that it was because of her religious beliefs, not for fashion. "Not true," she replied. "If I wanted to do that, I'd wear one with a little man on it."

BUT OF COURSE!

Returning from Crete, I commented that my
girlfriend's mate's suitcase was really heavy. Luckily
she had a solution: "If you repack everything neatly,
it'll weigh less."

FINAL FRONTIER

A news report said how they were going to stop servicing the Hubble Space Telescope after 14 years in orbit. "Does that mean the astronauts on board can finally come home?" asked the girlfriend. She's studying to be a doctor.

BE VERY AFRAID

After visiting the London Dungeons I told my girlfriend the story of Jack the Ripper. "Did they ever catch him?" she asked. I explained that they hadn't, but there had been many suspects. "Then he could still be wandering the streets of London today!" she gasped.

YOU HUM IT...

My girlfriend Christine was telling her mates about a
friend of mine who was on the England karate team,
only for one of them to ask, "What song does he sing?"

IF ONLY I COULD...

During a dispute with my mate about who was taller, my girlfriend made us stand back to back. When she declared that my mate was taller, I protested. "Come and have a look for yourself," she told me, calmly.

GOOD QUESTION

My female housemate recently tried to solve a query that had clearly been bothering her for some time. "You know nipples?" she asked, puzzled. "What are they called on men?" This from a woman allegedly studying law!

WELL, THEY MIGHT DO!

When my girlfriend was learning to drive, she was asked, "What do you need to watch for falling off the trees in autumn?" Her reply: "Squirrels." She's a copper, by the way.

TWELFH MAN

I took my girlfriend for her first experience of watching football at the pub. The place was packed and all was going well, until Tony Adams put his hand on the mascot's shoulder. "What position does that little man play in?" she asked, loudly.

APPLIANCE OF SCIENCE

My brother was cooking some lunch when my girlfriend asked whether you could get "reverse-microwaves, to make things colder?" Er… like a fridge?

SUB-STANDARD

A girl I know was showing me the "Stars & Stripes" bikini she'd bought for her Australian holiday. I said it was a shame she wasn't going to the US. "Don't worry," she told me, "Australia uses the same flag." She qualifies as a doctor in ten months.

CAPISCE?

My ex saw *The Godfather* and was halfway through the second one before asking, "Is Michael Corleone something to do with the Mafia?"

ACCIDENT OF HISTORY

Visiting the place where Irish martyr Michael Collins was shot, my sister asked why he didn't take cover behind the memorial when they were shooting at him.

KNOCK IT ON THE HEAD

Taking my wife fishing for the first time, I had no bites at all – so she decided to have a go. Minutes later she was reeling in a 3½ lb trout. "Aren't they supposed to be dead when you catch them?" she screamed, then watched horrified as I beat its little head in with a hammer. That was her final angling experience.

INSPIRING REMARK

While taking the last of her three daily inhalers, my girlfriend exclaimed, "I seem to spend half my life just breathing in!"

F AS IN 'FICK'

Surfing the internet, I asked my girlfriend to go to the *FHM* website. She paused before asking, "How do you spell *FHM*?" Oh – and she's studying for a degree!

OCH AYE THE NOO

My Scottish mate had just become a dad, and joked that his little boy would probably end up with his huge conk and flat feet. "Will he inherit your accent, or will he speak English like your wife?" queried my girlfriend, in all seriousness.

UNNATURAL VIOLENCE

My mate was recently telling his girlfriend about an acquaintance who'd been badly beaten up and had staples in his head. "Christ!" she retorted, obviously shocked. "Why would anyone attack someone with a stapler?"

DON'T MAKE ME ANGRY

Discussing *The Incredible Hulk* TV series one lunchtime, we established that Dr David Banner was played by Bill Bixby and the Hulk by Lou Ferrigno. The office blonde chipped in, "Was it two different actors, then?"

ROOM 101

While discussing how shit *Big Brother* was, my
flatmate quipped, "If only it were more like the 1984
version…" His girlfriend replied, "Was that the first
series, then?"

BACK FOR DINNER

On holiday in Woolacombe, my girl, noticing a small island off the bay, declared that it would be nice to walk there when the tide was out. The island in question, Lundy, was at least 30 miles off the coast.

LOOSE FLAPS OF SKIN

When an otter appeared on the TV, my female flatmate said, "Otters are the ones that fly, aren't they?" After we'd stopped laughing, she qualified her statement. "Well, they don't really fly – they glide."

NOT YOUR THING

A female friend of mine was shown a blow-up sex doll at a party. Noticing the rounded, cavernous mouth, she blurted out: "Eeew! That wouldn't be very nice to kiss."

THERE'S A THOUGHT

Talking about a pet for our new flat, I suggested
a tortoise. My flatmate pointed out that tortoises
hibernate for half the year. "Why not get two, then?"
my girlfriend chipped in.

STEALTH TECHNOLOGY

Watching the news about the *Ark Royal* departing for the Gulf, the commentator said that the ship was carrying, amongst other weaponry, Merlin anti-submarine helicopters. "Does that mean they fly underwater?" asked my girlfriend.

I'M ON A DIET

Out for a meal, my mother-in-law was asked by the waiter whether she wanted her pizza cut into four or six slices. "Four," she said. "I couldn't possibly manage six."

BUMMER, DUDE

The pub conversation got round to the subject of anal sex. "I couldn't be doing with that," said my mate's girlfriend. "I'd need more than one bonk a year."

IN THE STARS

My lady and I were having a Chinese when we heard people talking about being born in the Year of the Rat. Asked if she knew what year she'd been born in, she said, "'Course; 1978."

IT'S NOT REAL

On *Walking With Dinosaurs*, one of the creatures was dying on a beach, looking as if it was in extreme pain. "Can't the camera crew do anything to help?" my girlfriend piped up.

A KIND OF MAGIC

The other day at the fast-food outlet where I work, one of the girls washed her hands, then asked with a puzzled look, "How come these driers never run out of air? Have we received some on delivery?"

SOWING YOUR SEED

Watching a TV ad for Durex where men dressed up as sperm followed a bloke around, one of my female friends piped up: "What have spring onions got to do with condoms?"

I REMEMBER HIM

My mother-in-law was struggling with a celebrity crossword. "It's Sam somebody…" she said. I reeled off all the Sams I knew, to no avail. Then she said, "I've got it! Sam Anthamumba!"

IN-FLIGHT ENTERTAINMENT

While staying on the 24th floor of a Las Vegas hotel, my girlfriend was told by her mum to close the curtains while getting undressed – so passing aeroplane passengers "couldn't see in".

TASTE SENSATION

Watching an ad for Appletiser, the missus piped up with, "I like Appletiser, but it would be so much nicer if there was a non-fizzy version." That'll be apple juice.

SENSE OF DIRECTION

I caught my missus staring out of the window last week. "Which way is it that clouds go?" she asked. For 21 years, she'd thought clouds always moved in the same direction. Help!

UH-HUH-HUH

One cold morning in the office, I exclaimed, "It's like Greenland in here!" A female colleague looked up in confusion and said, "Isn't that where Elvis lived?"

THE SAME, ONLY DIFFERENT

After remarking to my mate's bird that it was nice to see the sun and the moon in the sky at the same time, she told me: "Don't be stupid! How can that happen? They're the same thing."

GEE, THANKS

My mum had a stroke and was told she would eventually lose her sight. My girlfriend was very upset, but had these words of consolation: "Don't worry – I'll learn Braille so I can read to you when you're blind."

UNCONSCIOUS SEXISM

On a trip to a park, my wife and I joined some schoolkids for a tour of the cow fields, where she raised her hand and asked, "Why do all of your cows have girls' names?"

IT REALLY HAPPENED

Watching TV, the film *Event Horizon* was coming up. My girlfriend asked what it was about. I explained it was set in the future, when some professor goes mental aboard a spaceship and kills people. "Is it a true story?" she said.

THEY'RE JUST NICER

Supermarket shopping with my beautiful girlfriend, I asked her to grab a pack of medium fresh eggs. With no response, I turned to see her staring puzzled at the shelves. "Can't we just get some fully fresh ones?" she asked.

ADAPT OR DIE

Watching a programme on turtles, my girlfriend became confused. "Are turtles born with shells on their back?" she burbled, "or do they need to find one?"

TIGHT FORMATION

Organising the Royal Naval Air Station Yeovilton International Air Day, I took a phone call from a lady asking if it was to be an indoor event. The Red Arrows were due to appear!

BUT IF YOU DID...

One of my housemates was preparing for a job interview and read out the list of perks. "Interest-free season ticket loan?" she queried. "But I don't even like football." Hair colour: blonde.

YOU KNOW WHAT I MEAN

While working as an office temp my sister had to type up an illegible handwritten letter which came from the County Chief Executive. Unfortunately, she used her "initiative" – and signed off his title as "Country Chef Executioner".

THAT'S A RELIEF

My wife rang me at work to tell me her car had a flat tyre. "But I don't think it's too bad," she said. "It's only flat at the bottom."

IT'S A BIT TECHNICAL

On the train recently with a female friend, she innocently asked, "How does the train-driver steer? Does he have a wheel, like in a car?" Despite seeing my look of utter disbelief, she ploughed on, "How does he change rails?"

DOES NOT COMPUTE

Watching football on the telly, a player was taking a throw-in. "What's that thing on his back?" asked my girlfriend. "Is it a backwards 'E'?" It was, of course, the number three. She's currently at the University of Newcastle, studying mathematics.

FIENDISH LOGIC

After hearing that the Pentagon had been attacked on 9/11, my girl assured me that Sheffield would be next on the hit-list. "We've got the Octagon…" she explained.

MINTED

My ex once got a letter from her bank, informing her she was badly overdrawn. "I'm not!" she wailed, waving her chequebook. "Look – I've got loads of cheques left."

PRACTICAL SUGGESTION

After a frozen car door incident, my then girlfriend bought me a can of de-icer. A few days later she came round and saw her present in the kitchen. "You should keep it in the glovebox of your car," she suggested. "Then it's always handy."